The World's Best Part-Time Job

Princeton Mayberry

DEDICATION

I would like to dedicate this book to the working class of the United States. Arguably the most important yet least understood and represented class. I understand the hard work and dedication we all have to endure to make a living and support our families. We single handedly built this beautiful country and this book is intended to enlighten you about the wonderful possibilities of making your money work just as hard as you.

CONTENTS

Acknowledgments   i

1   Introduction   Pg 1

2   Why Investing In The Stock Market Is Important   Pg 5

3   What Is Investing?   Pg 9

4   Reviewing A Stock & Bond   Pg 15

5   Risk Tolerance   Pg 21

6   Mystery Of The Stock Market Solved   Pg 24

7   Security Evaluation   Pg 28

8   Funds   Pg 40

9   Investment Strategies   Pg 45

10 Portfolio Allocation   Pg 68

11 Opening Your Brokerage Account   Pg 71

12 Processing Your First Investment   Pg 83

13 Employer Sponsored Retirement Accounts   Pg 89

14 Bringing It All Together & Extras   Pg 95

ACKNOWLEDGMENTS

I would like to take the time right now to thank all those who supported me and purchased the first edition of "Beginner Investing" which was my first publication. Without the support of you all I would not have been able to sum up the courage to continue to write and educate the working class on the benefits of the financial markets. A special thanks to all my mangers, directors, mentors and business associates. I would also like to thank my wife and kids for their continuous love and support.

I would like to also personally thank Yahoo for providing free Yahoo Finance services, Investopedia and the Chicago Board Option Exchange for the various free trainings and fundamental financial education information. I would like to thank the public library in Fresno County for providing access to various books, eBooks and tons of free services to further financial education and understanding in the community.

Finally I would like to thank you for not only this book but also reading this book. If you find one aspect or topic covered in the book useful, I urge you to share with family and friends and hopes that one day we all us working class citizens are financial independent and free to enjoy life to its fullest potential.

1 INTRODUCTION

What a wonderful time to be alive! Thanks to advancements in technology we are able to accomplish tasks at an alarming rate. More specifically the advancements in the stock market that allow anyone to set up an account to invest. You no longer need a broker or financial advisor to manage your finances. If you are interested in financial freedom, a sure path will be invested in your native and worldwide economies. It would be a good idea for parents to teach their kids about the stock markets and how it can be used as a tool to build wealth..

The purpose of this book is to educate you on the basics of investing so that you can begin investing in the stock market to build wealth. There is an abundance of information that you can learn about the stock market, but that is not the focus of this book. I will inform you of the basic information needed to get started in the markets and build wealth.

The goal of this book is to empower individuals of the working class to become their own financial advisors by taking control of their finances and financial education. I want you to save the money you pay to an advisor to manage your investment account and instead manage it yourself. We will keep the investing strategy simple as possible. No one will manage your money better than you, so it is critical that you learn the basics of investing.

This book is for those who are interested in investing in the stock market but do not know how to start. What I am out to cause is to get you started in the market building lifetime wealth. Future books will go into strategies and other concepts outside of the main income building strategies I cover in this book. Let me preference that statement with the following; Building wealth will take some time. Unless you currently have an abundance of money to invest right now, most likely you will have to start your investing practices small and build up. This is not a "get rich quick" scheme. It will teach you the strategy you need to build wealth, which in my opinion is a life skill. Once you commit this process to memory and truly embrace it, financial independence is inevitable.

I will also be using examples from the U.S stock market, however all the strategies remain the same. Be sure to do your own research on any products, securities or companies that may be mentioned in this book before making any decisions. Remember the goal is to assist you with taking control of your financial future. None of the information cover in this book is to be taken as financial advice. Always remember to do your own research or consult a professional if you have any financial questions or need financial advice.

Upon completion of this book I invite you all to follow my blog "World's Best Part-Time Job" or join me on social media sites "LinkedIn" or "Instagram" for further discussions and information regarding the stock market. Remember this book is intended to get you started in the stock market. You definitely want to continue your financial education and research after reading this book.

2 WHY INVESTING IN THE STOCK MARKET IS IMPORTANT

The stock market is one of many different markets available in the economy. The stock market is perfect for beginner investors for several reasons. The most important reason being that you can passively invest, that is invest with little effort on your part. Also you can create a portfolio to reach any goal imaginable. It also requires the least amount of information to get started which you will learn in this book. The most important reason by far is that unlike real estate and other investment markets, the stock market is liquid.

An interesting fact is that assets will always be worth more than cash in the future. To understand this concept you need only understand the concept of inflation. As time progresses, the power of the U.S dollar become less while the price of goods and services increase. Essentially we have to spend more dollars than before for the same goods or services. With assets the general rule is that they increase in value over time. If you wish to hedge your cash, that is have insurance against inflation, you simply need to accumulate value increasing assets.

I would like you to think of the stock market as the workplace you are going to send your money to work. Your money's job is only to make more money. With this new money that your money made, you will simply send it to work with the same objective. This process repeat itself and that is how someone like Warren Buffet was able to change $400 dollars into over $250,000. Remember successful people invest in the markets with a goal. Do not get caught up trying to chase the success of other people in the market you may see on TV. Do pay attention to the principles they used to get there. As mentioned in the previous section, most of you may not have a couple of grand to start your investing career. Do not let that discourage you as the process not the outcome is the true lesson that needs to be learned.

The stock market is one of the places the wealthy build their wealth. This is where they maintain and pass on their wealth. The possibilities are endless. Do you have a dream of being a stay at home parent? Or do you hate the idea of a 9-5? If done correctly, the stock market can make those dreams reality. Realize this, once you have learned the life skill of investing you will be able to make money for the rest of your life. No college education, degree or certificate can make that same guarantee. Remember money is nothing more than a tool to acquire items we want in life. The stock market provides a platform to use this tool to build wealth.

So what is the stock market? It is nothing more than a place where buyers and sellers of publically traded companies meet to make their transactions. Today you can setup a brokerage account and perform all your trades from the privacy of your own home or smart phone. This book is for beginners, I will covering strategies that will have you earning money immediately. I have personally used the strategies covered in this book, again I do not guarantee you will achieve the same success I received utilizing the strategies. Upon mastery of these strategies please check out my website or blog for more advanced wealth building strategies.

3 WHAT IS INVESTING?

Investing is the act of committing money or capital to an endeavor with the expectation of obtaining additional income or profit. Investors intend to hold on to their stock for long periods of time to capture a profit as the stock mature or pay a dividend. You can purchase stocks or bonds for individual companies or you can invest in a fund that pools together multiple companies. We will only discuss the basic investment securities in this book.

Another option is trading. Trading is nothing more than short-term investing. Traders typically do not intend on holding on to stocks for long periods of time. They are after the quick gain, opposite of investors.

Trading stocks involves more of your time. It is geared towards the more intermediate to advanced market player. You essentially attempt to *time* the market. You may have heard someone say "buy low and sell high" for example. If you discover you have a real interest in actively being involved in the market with trading I suggest you pick up some books on trading and or follow my blog "World's Best Part-Time Job" as I break down graphs and provide trading strategies.

In this book we will only focus on investing. To be clear there are different types of investing but I will focus on income investing. As simple as it sounds, growth investing means you will invest in stocks that have growth potential. Income investing is an investment strategy that invests in securities that provide cash flow.

There are 13 basic investment types. Each type of investment has its own risk factors and strategies that can be used to meet your investment goals. *FINRA* (Financial Industry Regulatory Authority) which is a non-profit organization authorized by Congress to protect American investors, provides great descriptions of each as follows:

Stocks – When you buy shares of a company's stock, you own a piece of that company. Stocks come in a wide variety, and they often are described based on the company size, type and performance during market cycles and potential for short- and long-term growth.

Bonds – A bond is a loan an investor makes to an organization in exchange for interest payments over a specified term plus repayment of principal at the bonds maturity date.

Investment Funds – Funds such as mutual funds, closed-end funds and exchange traded funds, pool money from many investors and invest it according to a specific investment strategy. Funds can offer diversification, professional management and a wide variety of investment strategies and styles.

Bank Products – Banks and credit unions can provide a safe and convenient way to accumulate savings and some banks offer services that can help you manage your money. Checking and savings accounts offer liquidity and flexibility.

Options – Options are contracts that give

the purchaser the right, but not the obligation to buy or sell a security, such as a stock or exchange traded fund at a fixed price within a specific period of time.

Annuities – An annuity is a contract between you and an insurance company in which the company promises to make periodic payments either starting immediately or at some future time.

Retirement – Numerous types of investments come into play when saving for retirement and managing income once you retire. For saving, tax-advantaged retirement options such as 401(k) or an IRA (individual retirement account) can be a smart choice. Managing retirement income may require moving out of certain investments and into ones that are better suited to a retirement lifestyle.

Saving For College – Funding College begins with savings, starting with how much to save. including 529 college savings plans and Coverdell Education Savings Accounts.

Alternative & Complex Products- These products include notes with principal protection and high-yield bonds that have lower credit rating and higher risk of default than traditional investments, but offer more attractive rates of return.

Initial Coin Offerings & Cryptocurrencies – These are speculative investments that come with significant uncertainty and many risks.

Commodity Futures – Commodity futures contracts are agreements to buy or sell a specific quantity of a commodity at a specified price on a particular date in the future. Commodities include metals, oil, grains and animal products as well as financial instruments and currencies. With limited exceptions, trading in futures contracts must be executed on the floor of a commodity exchange.

Security Futures – Federal regulations permit trading in futures contracts on single stocks, also known as single stock futures and certain security indices.

Insurance – Life insurance products come in various forms, including term life, whole life and universal life policies. There are variations on these, variable life insurance and variable universal life which are considered securities.

The bulk of this book will focus on strategies that will utilize the stock, bonds, option and investment funds categories.

4 REVIEWING A STOCK & BOND

Below you will find some definitions you should commit to memory.

- Asset: Anything of value that can be converted into cash.
- Stock: A type of security that signifies ownership in a corporation and represents a claim on part of the corporation's assets and earnings.
- Bond: A fixed income investment in which an investor loans money to an entity which borrows the funds for a set period of time at a variable or fixed interest rate.
- Fund: A supply of capital belonging to numerous investors used to collectively purchase securities while each investor retains ownership and control of his own shares.

- Exchange-Traded Fund: A marketable security that tracks an index, a commodity, bonds, or a basket of assets like an index fund.
- Mutual Fund: An investment vehicle made up of a pool of monies collected from many investors for the purpose of investing in securities such as stocks, bonds and other assets.
- Portfolio: A grouping of financial assets.
- Stock Market: Collection of markets and exchanges where the issuing and trading of equities or stocks of publicly held companies, bonds, and other classes of securities takes place.
- Brokerage Account: An arrangement between an investor and a licensed brokerage firm permitting the investor to deposit funds with the firm and place investment orders through the brokerage.
- Unrealized Gain: A profit that exists on paper, resulting from an investment.
- Ask & Bid Price: The current ask (sell) price for a stock & bid (buy) price for a stock.
- REIT: Real estate investment trust.
- Security Screener: Tool used to search for financial instruments.

- Dollar Cost Averaging: An investor places a fixed dollar amount into a given investment on a regular basis.
- Volatility: Measure of the dispersion of returns for a given security.

Now that you have some of the basic terminology down, let's take a look at a stock. Below you will find the stock for Facebook. Images provided by *Yahoo Finance*

Figure 1

Figure 2

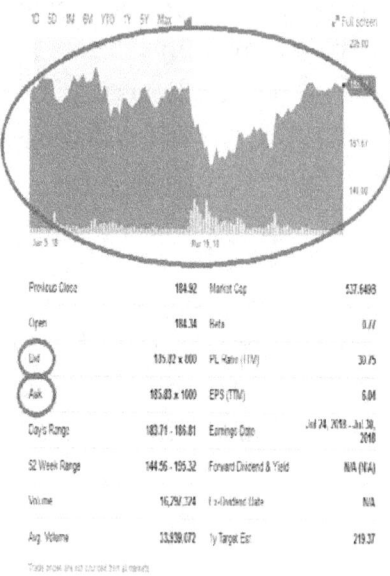

Figure 1. Reveals all the basic information you need about the stock. You will find the name, ticker, current price and closing price. You will also see numbers next to the price highlighted green if price movement is positive or red if movement is negative. Figure 2. Represents a visual representation of the same price movement. This graph shows you the closing price of Facebook dating back to the beginning of 2018. As you can see this stock has increased in price by roughly a dollar. What that means to you is that for every Facebook stock you own, they have now increased in value by $1. For example if

you own 100 Facebook stocks, you earned $100 cash value on your stock. Note: At this point the increased value of your Facebook stock is known as a capital gain as you have not sold the stock to realize the profit.

Also pay attention to the EPS number which stands for earnings per share. This number is important for long term investing as it indicates what you can expect to earn for each stock you own in the company. The PE ratio which stands for price earnings ratio is equally important for the same reason. This ratio shows you how much the price of the stock is selling for based on its earnings. Often stocks can be selling for more than they are earning (inflated price). These situations are a result of sellers driving up the price of the stock based on any number of reasons. Eventually the stock will self-correct and return to its correct price based on its earning potential. So be careful of "jumping on the bandwagon" of hot selling stocks as they may be on their way to a serious price correction. If you multiply these two numbers you will get the current price of the stock. So our example would read as: Facebook is currently selling for 30.75 times it's earnings of 6.04 earnings per share.

I also circled the current ask and bid price for the stock. The bid price is the price buyers are willing to pay to buy the stock, the ask price is the amount sellers are willing to sale the stock. The rest of the information you need not worry about at this stage in your investment career. It is a good practice to be able to understand the basic information regarding stocks. The information for bonds will be presented in the same format but require a different understanding. As none of the strategies mentioned in this book utilize bonds, I will not go into detail regarding bonds. At this point I would like you to get some practice looking at some stock. Head over to *Yahoo Finance* and look up the following stocks. The information for bonds will be presented in the same format.

- General Motors
- Amazon
- Netflix

5 RISK TOLERANCE

When it comes to investing, rather it be age, lifestyle or even culture; we all have various risks levels. Some of you may be on the extreme ends of the spectrum. For example; you may not be willing to risk a dime while others may be willing to risk it all. More importantly is how to determine where you fall in the spectrum. To determine this I suggest you answer this simple question, how much of dollar would you risk to make another one?

The more of your dollar you are willing to risk the higher your risk level. Extreme risk takers are willing to risk their entire investment while extremely low risk takers are willing to risk next to nothing. Now that you have a better idea of how risk factor effects the type of allocation you should have, you can understand why there is no magical *"one fit all"* allocation. Everybody will have different investment goals, therefore everybody's portfolio allocation will be different.

Your risk factor relates to your investment portfolio in the following way. If you are risky then you may consider a more equity weighted portfolio allocation. The less risky may consider an allocation consisting of fixed income securities and money market instruments. Remember there is no right or wrong way to build your portfolio. Your focus should always be to construct a portfolio that will meet your personal goals.

Think of the rest of this book as your personal financial advisor. It has been my experience that a basic income generation and preservation portfolio is ideal for the risk level of the new investor. Some financial experts may attempt to get you to believe the more risk you take the better your return will be which is not always the case. While some may have a longer time horizon to build wealth that does not mean that person should expose themselves to unnecessary risks and potential losses.

6 MYSTERY OF THE STOCK
MARKET SOLVED

Millions of people lose countless amount of money in the stock market every year. Do you know who is on the receiving end of all that extra cash? You guessed it the professionals. What do the professionals know that the average investors do not? Please allow me to provide my insight on the concept.

In order to make real money in the stock market you must understand how it works. Remember, the stock market only goes up when people are buying, that is to say only when new money is being added into the market. Some of the biggest contributions of this new money is through employer sponsored retirement accounts for instance. For example, you own shares in the mutual fund that hosts your retirement account. At times you will experience capital gains. The problem is that it is a capital gain which means it is a gain that is only recognized on paper. The problem is then that the average investor invests for capital gains, the professionals invest for cash flow. And by the way, you will still pay the fee your portfolio manager charges for managing the fund no matter what.

The professionals understand that in order to obtain wealth they cannot rely on capital gains. Instead they use strategies that provide them with cash flow. When there is an influx of money into a particular sector or market class that is the signal for traders to set their positions. As the stock grows in value based on the buying, the PE ratio (price earnings ratio) becomes inflated. These professionals then sale off their positions and realize that gain in their account. Notice they do not hold onto the stock, remember you can only recognize a capital gain by selling the stock. Meanwhile the average investor who belongs to the mutual fund experienced the same capital gain only to see it disappear and sometime worst by losing money when the selling begins. This is just one of the many opportunities that exist that allow the professionals to make money in the market. They feed on the intake of the new money into the market that is they are short term investors. The average person who is invested with a mutual fund via their retirement account is invested in the long term. Unfortunately your account will experience the rise of the capital gains only to see them swallowed up by the short term investor. So does that mean all mutual funds are bad and you should stay away from them? No, but what I am saying is that you must use the professional's strategy to choose the best investment instrument that provide you with the best opportunity to reach your investment goals.

I would also like to note that stocks typically trade in a range. Rarely will you see them break these support and resistance lines, and when they do that is typically a sign of a trend starting or reversing. Checkout the chapter "Security Evaluation" to learn two different methods for analyzing stocks. So when we hold onto stocks we are long term investors so it would be wise that we choose securities with above average financial history. You too can enjoy the passive income that the stock market has to offer. I will introduce you to three professional strategies. 1. Dividend Chaser, 2. Digital Real Estate Investor and 3. Paper Houses. All these strategies invest for cash flow. These methods will ensure you are investing on the side of the professionals not the amateurs. I list them in order of difficulty to manage and involvement required on behalf of the investor. I suggest you start at level one, master and move on to the next level. Depending on your investment goal, you can pick one strategy to construct your portfolio. Before we discuss the strategies, let's cover the methods for analyzing stocks.

7 SECURITY EVALUATION

When it comes to selecting the securities that will make up your portfolio, how do you know which securities to choose? While there may be several different methods available, I am going to introduce you to the two most popular. *Technical Analysis* and *Fundamental Analysis*.

Technical Analysis

Technical analysis is an investment method used to identify investment opportunities by analyzing statistical trends gathered from trading activity such as price movement and volume. For individuals that are in-tune with their senses, this may be the method for you. This method involves the use of graphs, indicators and the like in order to make a decision on the direction of the price of the security. The users of technical analysis aim to time the market. They base their investment decisions on what they see in the graphs of the price movement. Those of you who are visual learners may find this process effective as well as you can visually see the price movement on the charts. Let's review some important terms you will need to get familiar with if you choose to use this method.

- Technical Analysis – Technical Analysis is the practice of anticipating price changes of a financial instrument by analyzing prior price changes and looking for patterns and relations in price history. Technical events occur when a significant pattern has formed or a significant price activity has occurred in a financial instrument. Technical events highlight price situations that may be worth considering in researching an investment activity. Technical events can be used by investors to make more informed decisions about when to: Enter a new position, Close an existing position or wait for a better time to take action.

- Bearish – The term bearish refers to falling prices.

- Bullish – The term bullish refers to rising prices.

- Breakout – A rise in a security's price above a resistance level (usually its previous high) or a drop below a support level (usually its previous low).

- Indicator – This is a technical event category

- Index – A grouping of stocks used by the financial markets as a benchmark of performance.

- Resistance Line – A price level at which there would be sufficient sell order to slow or reverse an upward price movement.

- Support Line – A price level at which

there would be sufficient buy orders to slow or even reverse a downward price movement.

- Moving Average – A widely used indicator that helps smooth out price action by filtering out the random price fluctuations.

- Uptrend – Describes the price movement of a financial asset when the overall direction is upward

- Downtrend – Describes the price movement of a financial asset when the overall direction is downward.

- Sideways Trend – A trend that is the result of horizontal price movement based on the forces of supply and demand nearly being equal.

Send example of these trends below:

The preceding terms are not all the terms that are involved in technical analysis, however they are the most important terms for a beginner to understand. Let's take a look at a stock utilizing technical analysis and see if we can predict its movement. Then let's determine if we would like to invest in the security.

As you can see this is a year to date chart of the price movement of the security. The green horizontal line (32.21) represents the resistance line, the blue line (28.85) represents the support line. To recap the importance of these lines, the resistance line represents the average highest price movement within our selected range. The support line would represent the average lowest price movement within our selected range. Next notice the bars at the bottom of the graph. They represent the volume of the trade activity in millions.

The current price on the security is 30.33

which is about in the middle of our support and resistance lines. It appears that the price of security experienced a huge drop in the price as the volume spikes indicate. Perhaps a news announcement came out that day or maybe the company made an announcement to the public that wasn't so great. Whatever the situation may be, the price of the stock was definitely effected. The security is currently trading for the least amount it has traded in over the last year, but we can see that it did reach as high as 39 dollars in February. If we consider the big picture, that is the entire duration of the graph, the security is currently in a downtrend. With that being said, I would not invest in this security as of today. I never recommend any of my clients to invest in any security that is in a downtrend. How do you know when the downtrend has reached its bottom? If you are looking to get a great company at a discount, what if you are buying too early and experience unnecessary losses? What if the downtrend doesn't end? These are just some of the reasons why I recommend you stay away from investing in securities in a downtrend. There are strategies that take advantage of falling prices that are not discussed in this book as they require more risk on the behalf of the investor.

So would you invest in this security? If so why? If not, then why not? I want you to understand there is no right or wrong answer here. The point is for you to make a decision based on what you see. Based on this particular screenshot in time, what do you think the price will do next? If this type of analysis sounds like too much to bare for you, then maybe you should try fundamental analysis.

Fundamental Analysis

Fundamental analysis involves reviewing the financial documents of potential investment companies. You should look at the income statement, balance sheet and cash flow statement at a minimum. This type of analysis is number driven, if you love numbers you will find this type of analysis pleasing. For those of you who may not have looked at any financial statements or know what they are, let's start off with some terms you will need to be familiar with.

Income Statement (profit and loss) – Financial statement that shows a company's revenues and expenses during a particular period.

Balance Sheet – Financial statement that lists financial balance of a company as in assets, liabilities, owner and stockholder equity.

Cash Flow Statement – Financial statement that summarizes the amount of cash and cash equivalents entering and leaving a company.

The financial statements come in all different kinds of shapes and sizes but the information they represent remains the same. I suggest you look at 100 financial statements to get a good understanding of what they represent and grasp what the numbers mean to you as an investor. Let's look at a few of the statements

provided by *Yahoo Finance.*

Income Statement All numbers in thousands

Revenue	12/31/2017	12/31/2016	12/31/2015	12/31/2014
Total Revenue	160,546,000	163,786,000	146,801,000	132,447,000
Cost of Revenue	77,379,000	76,884,000	67,046,000	59,360,000
Gross Profit	**83,167,000**	**86,902,000**	**79,755,000**	**73,087,000**
Operating Expenses				
Research Development	-	-	-	-
Selling General and Administrative	34,917,000	36,003,000	32,544,000	39,697,000
Non Recurring	-	-	-	-
Others	-	-	-	-
Total Operating Expenses	136,683,000	138,734,000	121,606,000	117,330,000
Operating Income or Loss	**23,863,000**	**25,052,000**	**25,195,000**	**15,117,000**

Income from Continuing Operations

Balance Sheet All numbers in thousands

Period Ending	12/31/2017	12/31/2016	12/31/2015	12/31/2014
Current Assets				
Cash And Cash Equivalents	50,498,000	5,768,000	5,121,000	8,603,000
Short Term Investments	1,000	-	-	-
Net Receivables	18,303,000	18,400,000	18,304,000	14,527,000
Inventory	2,225,000	2,039,000	4,033,000	1,933,000
Other Current Assets	6,750,000	10,567,000	7,462,000	7,712,000
Total Current Assets	**79,146,000**	**38,369,000**	**35,992,000**	**33,606,000**
Long Term Investments	2,292,000	1,674,000	1,608,000	255,000
Property Plant and Equipment	125,222,000	124,899,000	124,450,000	112,898,000
Goodwill	105,449,000	105,207,000	104,568,000	69,692,000
Intangible Assets	114,276,000	116,860,000	120,710,000	66,963,000
Accumulated Amortization	-	-	-	-

Cash Flow (in thousands)   Annual | Quarterly

Period Ending	12/31/2017	12/31/2016	12/31/2015	12/31/2014
Net Income	29,450,000	12,976,000	13,345,000	6,442,000
Operating Activities, Cash Flows Provided By or Used In				
Depreciation	21,577,000	23,485,000	20,356,000	16,769,000
Adjustments To Net Income	-12,054,000	2,633,000	4,777,000	11,414,000
Changes In Accounts Receivables	-988,000	-1,003,000	30,000	-693,000
Changes In Liabilities	818,000	118,000	1,354,000	2,310,000
Changes In Inventories	-	-	-	-
Changes In Other Operating Activities	-2,462,000	-1,227,000	-5,642,000	-6,408,000
Total Cash Flow From Operating Activities	39,151,000	39,344,000	35,880,000	31,338,000
Investing Activities, Cash Flows Provided By or Used In				
Capital Expenditures	-21,955,000	-22,408,000	-20,015,000	-21,433,000
Investments	-4,000	506,000	1,545,000	3,995,000

Learning to read these statements will give
you a great understanding of a company's
financial state. You rely less on your senses
and more on facts and numbers. Being able to
see a company from the inside out will
provide you with valuable information you
need as an investor, especially for mid to long
term investment goals. As your research skills
advance, you will be able to find those special
companies that the average investor will miss.
You will be in the forefront of great value and
growth investment opportunities. Understand
this, successful American company "Amazon"
was selling for less than two dollars in 1997,

which is now selling for 1665.53 a share now and still rising. For research purposes, take a look at Amazon's financial statements from 1997. Would you have invested in their stock based on the numbers?

8 FUNDS

Utilizing some of the strategies in this book will require investment in a financial fund. Let's review some of the basic funds of the financial market. A book can be written on each of these type of investment funds to cover all the information about them. I will only cover key aspects as they relate to the investment strategies of this book.

Mutual Fund

A mutual fund is a professional managed investment fund that pools money from many investors to purchase securities. That saves you time on evaluating stocks and bonds as it has been done for you already.

Mutual funds allow you to invest in dollar amount value. Stocks, bonds and other funds only allow investment by share price. This is especially important for beginner investors who do not have a lot of capital to start their investing.

Select mutual funds are now available that do not charge any load fees. Whenever you buy a stock your brokerage firm typically will charge you a fee, with mutual funds there is typically no fee so more money for your investment. Be advised that the financial industry is constantly changing, so by the time you are reading this material the fee structure for investment instruments may have changed. Always check with your broker for the most recent information.

There is now a mutual fund for just about any and every investment sector. Rather you arc looking to invest in bonds, stocks, cash equivalents or even specific sectors like technology, financial and utilities.

Exchange Traded Fund

An exchange traded fund (ETF) is an investment fund that tracks a stock index, a commodity, bonds or a collection of assets. A major difference between mutual funds and exchange traded funds is that exchange traded funds trade like common stock on the stock exchange. The fees for ETFs are typically lower than mutual funds. From a tax standpoint ETFs are more beneficial to investors than mutual funds.

Exchange traded funds also have lower expense ratios. The expense ratio is the total percentage of fund assets used for administrative, management, advertising and other expenses. With exchange traded funds you can get the diversification of an index fund at a fraction of the cost. For example the current price of the S&P 500 (^GSPC) is 2723.06, exchange traded fund SPDR (SPY) that tracks the same index (^GSPC) is currently 271.89. So in essence you get the same benefits for a fraction of the cost

(^GSPC is an index not a fund).

In many ways an ETF is a hybrid of a stock and a mutual fund, it has the attributes of both. Depending on your personal investment goals, an ETF, mutual fund or both may be needed to meet and exceed those goals. The last type of fund I would like to mention is a money market fund, please see definition below.

Money Market Fund – A type of fixed income mutual fund that only invests in highly liquid cash and cash equivalent securities that have high credit ratings. These funds invest primarily in debt-based securities which have short-term maturity of about a year.

9 INVESTING STRATEGIES

So what does it mean to be a passive investor? It is a "hands off" approach to investing or an investment strategy that requires minimal effort from the investor. This type of investor need not worry about keeping up with the news.

The next strategy requires more activity on behalf of the investor. This strategy will involve investing in real estate through a trust. We will invest in real estate investment trusts (REIT).

The final strategy is what I call paper houses. This requires the most involvement on the behalf of the investor however provides larger amount of monthly income for the additional work. These are proven strategies that the professional investors practice. A common misconception when it comes to investing strategies is that income investing is reserved for the conservative investor. Investing for income is reserved for people who are in retirement or near it, and need to generate the monthly income to survive. That my friends could not be further from the truth. Your ultimate goal is to make money. Never lose sight of this principle and use it to guide your investment decisions. Why wait until your retired or on the brink of retirement before you start earning passive income? Could you not benefit from that extra income right now in your late teens? 20s? 30s? 40s? A byproduct of your efficient investing utilizing these strategies will provide you with a few benefits.

One you would have built up a massive asset column. Two at a certain point in the future your passive income will surpass your earned income which will allow to quit your job or retire early, or simply keep the job and build your assets even faster. Three, unlike a 401k which is basically a savings account, you would have been earning cash the entire time on top of your initial investment. When you invest for income you are essentially investing for cash flow. I would like you to think of it as building a business that at a future date will provide you with a passive paycheck for the rest of your life. Sounds similar to an annuity right?

Dividend Chasing

The first investment strategy I would like to

share with you is what I call *dividend chasing*. As the names states, with this strategy we will be investing strictly to earn dividends. Some of the best dividend stocks will be utility companies, REITs and well managed companies that pay great dividends to its shareholders. I will reserve investing in REITs for our second investment strategy. Our goal is to build a portfolio of dividend providing securities. To keep things extremely simple we will setup a dividend mutual fund. The mutual fund will include all the stocks we described previously. One of the perks of using a mutual fund for this strategy is that certain mutual funds do not charge commission to buy shares. While there are multiple mutual funds to choose from, there is a limited amount of securities that compose these funds. You want to find a fund with no load fees and no commission chargers. For example if you use *Fidelity* as your brokerage they have a fund *"Fidelity's Equity Dividend Income Fund"*. It really is as simple as setting up a brokerage account, finding the mutual fund and buying shares into the mutual fund. Another positive is that you do not have to spend countless hours researching to hand select the securities, that is the responsibility of the professional portfolio manager.

Once you have set up your brokerage account and picked your mutual fund, I want you to adjust a few settings. First I want you to setup automatic withdrawal from your checking/saving account to your brokerage account. You decide how often and how much. Next from your brokerage account setup up automatic purchase of the mutual fund in the exact amount that is deposited into the account. Be sure to set the purchase date at least a week out from the deposit date as some banks take about a week for the funds to transfer. The last step is to setup automatic reinvest of dividends received from mutual fund. This means that the dividends you earn from the mutual fund will be used to grow your position in the mutual fund which in turn will increase the amount dividend you earn on future disbursements. Once a quarter review your position. As you can see all the work with this strategy is performed once at the beginning and you simply monitor thereafter and watch your money grow.

To initiate this strategy your first need to identify an income producing mutual fund that is a fund whose purpose is to generate income for its investors. A simple search using the mutual fund screener provided by *Yahoo Finance* will provide you with an abundance of mutual funds. Most brokerages provide their own investment products which are typically free of commission charges for their members.

☐	VEIPX	Vanguard Equity-Income Inv
☐	VISVX	Vanguard Small Cap Value Index Inv
☐	TRVLX	T. Rowe Price Value
☐	TRPIX	T. Rowe Price Value I
☐	LCEAX	Invesco Diversified Dividend A
☐	DFLVX	DFA US Large Cap Value I
☐	PAFDX	T. Rowe Price Equity Income Advisor
☐	REIPX	T. Rowe Price Equity Income I
☐	RRFDX	T. Rowe Price Equity Income R
☐	LCEYX	Invesco Diversified Dividend Y
☐	LCEFX	Invesco Diversified Dividend R6
☐	DDFRX	Invesco Diversified Dividend R
☐	MADVX	BlackRock Equity Dividend Instl
☐	BEDCX	BlackRock Equity Dividend Inv C1
☐	MKDVX	BlackRock Equity Dividend K
☐	MDDVX	BlackRock Equity Dividend Inv A

I suggest looking at either Vanguard or Fidelity mutual funds as they are typically investor friendly and have no front load fees.

VIVIX	Vanguard Value Index I	
VVIAX	Vanguard Value Index Adm	
VIVAX	Vanguard Value Index Inv	
VWNFX	Vanguard Windsor II Inv	
VWNAX	Vanguard Windsor II Admiral	
VEIRX	Vanguard Equity-Income Adm	
VSIIX	Vanguard Small Cap Value Index I	
VSIAX	Vanguard Small Cap Value Index Admiral	✔
VHDYX	Vanguard High Dividend Yield Index Inv	
VEIPX	Vanguard Equity-Income Inv	
VISVX	Vanguard Small Cap Value Index Inv	
VWNDX	Vanguard Windsor Inv	
VWNEX	Vanguard Windsor Admiral	

FSLEX	Fidelity Series Six Select Lg Cp Val	
FEQIX	Fidelity Equity-Income	
FEIKX	Fidelity Equity-Income K	
FNKLX	Fidelity Series Value Discovery	✔
FEQTX	Fidelity Equity Dividend Income	
FIOOX	Fidelity Series Large Cap Value Index	
FCVCX	Fidelity Advisor Small Cap Value C	
FCVIX	Fidelity Advisor Small Cap Value I	
FCPVX	Fidelity Small Cap Value	
FVDFX	Fidelity Value Discovery	
FLVEX	Fidelity Large Cap Value Enhanced Index	

Next within your brokerage account you will buy shares of this fund based on your investment goals. Remember to setup the automatic deposit of funds into your brokerage account and also the automatic investment into the mutual fund and you are done. Using this simple yet effective strategy you will be able to build financial wealth. It only requires minimal work from you initially to setup the accounts and settings. If you have never invested before this is where I recommend you start. I suggest you only make changes to this process bi-annually if any adjustment at all. If you receive a raise at work or just run into additional capital feel free to deposit the money into your brokerage account until you are ready to make the changes at your bi-annual interval, as your brokerage account will pay you a higher interest rate on your money than any bank savings account will offer.

REITs: The Digital Real Estate Investor

The digital real estate investor strategy is similar to that of the dividend chasing strategy as we are investing to receive dividends. The difference being that with this strategy we will be targeting only REITs (real estate investment trusts).

So what is a REIT? A real estate investment trust is a company that owns and in some cases operates income producing real estate. They own various different types of commercial real estate including but not limited to offices, apartment complexes, hospitals, shopping centers, hotels and warehouses.

So why are they important? Buying and selling real property can be a vigorous process. Involving many key players including but not limited to brokers, real estate agents, escrow, appraisers and inspectors. Depending on the type of building you own, you may also have to have a property management company assist you in the daily operation of the property. In most cases they involve a hefty down payment on the behalf of the purchaser and may require some form of a loan like a mortgage.

When you invest in a real estate investment trust, all those worries and processes go away. You simply buy shares in the company and enjoy your share of the profits. REITs are a great tool for beginner investors to leverage their money. For example, it may cost you ten thousand dollars for a down payment on a new rental property, now if you invest through a REIT instead, you can purchase shares for ten dollars (made up price for you to understand the logic) and not only share in the profits of that rental property but others that are owned by the trust. Remember your share of the profit is determined by the amount of shares you have in the REIT. For example let's say that XYZ REIT's current share price is one dollar and they currently pay a dividend of fifty cents. With your ten thousand dollars you can buy ten thousand shares of XYZ REIT and earn fifty cents a share. That equates to a five thousand dollar profit or a return on your investment of 50%. (10,000*.50=5,000. 5,000/10,000=0.5 or 50%)

XYZ REIT

Share Price: 1.00USD

Dividend: 0.50USD

You

Investment Balance: 10,000USD

# of Shares Purchased: 10,000

Dividend Payment: 5,000USD

Return On Investment: 50%

Another great benefit of real estate investment trusts is that they are required by law to distribute at least 90% of its profits to its investors, which is paid out in the form of a dividend. That is exactly what we are after, cash flow from our investments. Investment in REITs provides investors with a liquid ownership position in real estate.

Our strategy is to construct a portfolio of real estate investment trusts. Within our portfolio we will want to be sure to cover all

major sectors of the real estate industry. Now
you may be able to find one trust that includes
all the various types of real estate. I however
recommend that you split your holdings
among a few different trusts to hedge your
position. Using the equity screener provided
by *Yahoo Finance* I was able to find the
following trusts:

AMT	American Tower Corporation (REIT)		149.61
SPG	Simon Property Group, Inc.		179.76
PLD	Prologis, Inc.		64.43
BAM	Brookfield Asset Management Inc.		40.23
PSA	Public Storage		200.82
EQR	Equity Residential		64.84
AVB	AvalonBay Communities, Inc.		174.89
DLR	Digital Realty Trust, Inc.		106.01
VTR	Ventas, Inc.		56.79
BXP	Boston Properties, Inc.		114.91
O	Realty Income Corporation		59.73
ESS	Essex Property Trust, Inc.		247.91
BPY	Brookfield Property Partners L.P.		18.88
HST	Host Hotels & Resorts, Inc		18.43
VNO	Vornado Realty Trust		67.02

As you can see there are no shortage of
trusts you can choose for your investment
portfolio. It would be wise to choose trusts
that focus specifically on certain sectors in real
estate. For instance if you were looking to

invest hotels, you may consider looking into Host Hotels & Resorts Inc from the list above. You can apply my hands off approach to the REIT investment strategy by instead of investing in individual trusts, invest in a mutual fund that pools them altogether.

☐	VGSIX	Vanguard Real Estate Index Investor
☐	VGSNX	Vanguard Real Estate Index Institutional
☐	DFREX	DFA Real Estate Securities I
☐	PAREX	T. Rowe Price Real Estate Advisor
☐	TIRRX	T. Rowe Price Real Estate I
☐	FRIOX	Fidelity Advisor Real Estate Income C
☐	FRIRX	Fidelity Advisor Real Estate Income I
☐	FRIQX	Fidelity Advisor Real Estate Income M
☐	FRIFX	Fidelity Real Estate Income
☐	CSRSX	Cohen & Steers Realty Shares
☐	FRSSX	Nuveen Real Estate Securities R3
☐	FARCX	Nuveen Real Estate Securities I
☐	CSCIX	Cohen & Steers Real Estate Securities C
☐	FRESX	Fidelity Real Estate Investment Port
☐	FRLCX	Nuveen Real Estate Securities C

It is a good idea to cover the main real estate categories including rental properties, health buildings, office spaces and shopping centers. Take note to the time table that each trust pays its dividend. It will be either annually, biannually, quarterly or monthly. Create a combination of the four to ensure constant cash flow into your real estate portfolio year around.

Paper Houses

The next strategy is for the investor who would like to be more involved and generate a higher rate of return. I would consider this an intermediate-advance level of investing. I created this strategy specifically for those who may even be interested in real estate investing. After reviewing the process you will see why I call it paper houses.

First let me briefly explain how traditional real estate investing works. In its simplest terms, you purchase a real property and lease the property to a tenant that pays you rent. The rent becomes your cash flow or return on investment. From this rent you pay any applicable liabilities of the property and what is leftover is your monthly profit. So what if we can take this simple process and apply it to the stock market, that is buy some stock, lease the stock out and keep the lease payment as your return on your investment. There is a process available to do just that, with the use of options.

To understand the process behind paper houses a brief explanation of options is needed. I believe *Investopedia.com* provides a great definition that states: *Options are a financial derivative sold by an option writer to an option buyer. The contract offers the buyer the right, but not the obligation, to buy (call option) or sell (put option) the underlying asset at an agreed-upon price during a certain period of time or on a specific date.* We will be selling option contracts to individuals for a fee, stated a different way, we will be leasing our stock to investors. At the end of the lease term we will repeat the process with another investor.

As you can see the process is simple enough, yet requires on your part precise selection of the stock you wish to lease out. To better understand the underlying process of paper houses I will provide you with some definitions regarding options.

All options are built on the following aspects:

- Call Option: Gives its holder the right

to buy stock at set price in the future.

- Put Option: Gives its holder the right to sell a stock at a set price in the future.

Our strategy will focus specifically on selling call options, more importantly a covered call option which means you own the stock and will lease it out for a premium with a set expiration date. The amount of the premium you collect and the expiration date will be vital to the success of this strategy. The market allows for weekly, monthly and sometimes yearly expiration dates with varying premiums.

So what can go wrong with this strategy? Worst case scenario is that you will have to sale your stock to the option contract holder and forfeit any capital gain on the stock. Please note that even if you do have to sell your stock it will be at a higher price than you paid for it so you will receive money from both the sale of the stock and collection of the premium. We simply would look for another stock that meet our qualifications and start the process again. You can also wait until the price of the sold stock goes down or even buy it at the higher cost.

Our best case scenario is that the option contract expires unexercised, we keep our stock and the premium... So what is the criteria for our paper house? When working with real property the saying goes "location is everything", with our paper house volatility and dividend yield top the list.

First we will only choose stocks that have a history of low volatility. This means the swings in price of the stock are not far from the current price of the stock. Options by design are leveraged financial derivatives, a slight move in price can be troublesome for option writers. If you choose a stock that experience a ton price spikes the chances of your stock option contract being exercised by the holder greatly increases. We prefer a stock that has moderate to low volatility simply to increase our odds of keeping our stock.

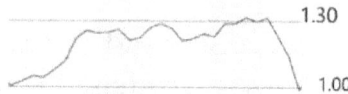

Take a look at the graph of a XYZ stock price movement from a previous month. From this picture we can see that the stock traded in a range from one dollar to one dollar thirty cents. As you can see there are no major peaks above the 1.30 range, also there are few to no dips below the 1 range. So from this information we can conclude that XYZ stock volatility, at least for the previous month was moderate to low. We then can assume that this volatility will continue into the next month but is not guaranteed, that is part of the risk built into the stock market; past performance does not guarantee future results. So using our paper house investment strategy, we would not sell any option contracts within the 1-1.30 range as the probability of it being in the range by the end of the lease period is high. We would sell option contracts at a price above 1.30.

The next factor would be choosing stock that also pay decent dividends. Dividends are important because they provide another stream of cash flow. The stock market, much like the real estate market moves in cycles. There are times when no one is looking to buy real estate, the same is true for stock. So to hedge our position we will only choose stocks that also pay a decent dividend. That way even if we are not able to make money renting out the stock, we will still experience cash flow in the form of dividends. As the saying go "I rather have a little of something than all of nothing". To recap on the income generation on this strategy, we receive cash flow from the premium we charge for others to rent our stock, we receive dividends as shareholders of the company and lastly we have the opportunity for capital gain if we are forced to sell our stock.

Our starting point will be to accumulate 100 shares of stock. Options are typically sold as one contract that equals 100 shares of the underlying stock. So to build your first paper house you will need to acquire 100 shares. For some of you this may be accomplished with the click of your mouse, for others you may have to make a few purchases to get to this point. Either way before purchasing the stock, take a look at its current price relative to the last 52 weeks. Review the price for any potential trends that may be in your favor. A current downtrend provides you with an opportunity to purchase your desired stock at a discount. These opportunities do not come along often so I suggest putting some cash aside in a money market account for this purpose.

I understand it is important to provide you with a stock that would meet all the qualifications recently discussed. As of today while I am writing this book, AT&T (stock ticker T) would qualify as a paper house. They currently have an annual dividend of 2.00 and have moderate volatility. The current asking price is 30.20 which means an investment of 3020.00usd is required to build a house.

Your next step is to review the current rent price (premium), to do that we need to look up the option chain for AT&T. I suggest *Chicago Board Option Exchange*, see below.

T(AT&T INC) Options Chain

Exchange: Cboe ▼

Oct 25, 2018 @ 15:18 ET

Bid: 30.15   Ask: 30.16   S:

Calls

OCTOBER 2018 (EXPIRATION: 10/26)

Strike	Last	Net	Bid	Ask	Vol	Int
T1826J29.5-E	0.55	+0.12	0.65	0.72	20	49
T1826J30-E	0.27	-0.28	0.25	0.30	1208	543
T1826J30.5-E	0.05	-0.25	0.05	0.07	404	1804
T1826J31-E	0.02	-0.11	0.0	0.15	308	2952

Calls

NOVEMBER 2018 (EXPIRATION: 11/02)

Strike	Last	Net	Bid	Ask	Vol	Int
T1802K29.5-E	1.16	-1.80	0.79	0.88	4	396
T1802K30-E	0.49	-0.26	0.46	0.50	47	329
T1802K30.5-E	0.23	-0.30	0.23	0.29	388	403
T1802K31-E	0.11	-0.21	0.10	0.13	543	1017

First let us review the seven columns starting with the strike column. The strike column represents that amount you will be paid per share if you have to sell your house. Remember this only occurs if the contract holder chooses to exercise their right. The "last" column indicates the price the last contract sold for at that particular strike price. The "net" column indicates the net change value based on the recent activity of that particular strike price. Next you have the bid and ask columns which are the same as the bid and ask columns of a stock we covered in a previous section. Next you have the volume column which lists the current outstanding contracts for that strike price. Lastly we have the "int" column or interest column which represents the current interest that strike price is yielding.

We will focus on the circled strike price. 29.5 represents the price at which you would have to sell your house per share if the option contract holder exercises their right. Remember the price is currently at 30.20 so from an option contractor writer view this would not be ideal. Simply looking at the different prices listed which would you consider writing an option contract for? As you may have noticed the farther you go away from the current price of the stock upwards, the option contract price decrease. Why is that?

A call option is only valuable to the contact holder if the price of the stock goes above the strike price. If you remember from our qualifications, we only wanted to choose stocks that experienced moderate to low volatility. As such this lack of price movement suggests the odds of the price going much above the current price as not likely. Thus the price of option contracts with prices much higher than the current price of the underlying stock will be low, as it is not likely the stock will reach that price. Now does that mean it will not happen? No but it is not likely.

So then the question becomes how far above the stock price should you select? The answer is somewhere in between. Choosing a price to low may result in a higher rent collected, but also an increase in the probability of the contract being executed... My suggestion is when starting out always choose a price that is farther rather than closer to the underlying stock price. That way you still collect rent and get to learn the process at the same time, as mentioned earlier, I rather have a little bit of something than all of nothing. Once you have gained experience with paper houses and selecting manageable strike prices you can focus on adding more paper houses or simply increasing the size of your current house. For beginners I suggest increasing the size of your current house as additional houses will require additional tracking. Remember the goal is to keep it simple. If you follow this process you can build a massive portfolio of paper houses that rival income created by real property. You get the benefits of the cash flow, without the headache of property management.

The World's Best Part-Time Job

10 PORTFOLIO ALLOCATIONS

A portfolio is all the securities you currently hold in your account. The allocation refers to the types of securities you hold in your account and to what percentage. The cardinal rule of your portfolio is to always achieve diversification. You never want to be overextended in any particular market or class unless that is the strategy that will help you meet your goal.

Do not be afraid to construct a portfolio that is intended to meet your goals. The term diversify is an overused and misunderstood term when it comes to portfolio allocations. Remember the purpose of diversification is to hedge your portfolio, that is, insurance just in case the stocks you picked turns out to cost you money and you're left in a losing position.

If starting out and you do not have a goal but would like to start investing, your portfolio should consist of nothing but government-backed bonds. You are guaranteed the interest payments during the course of the loan and receive your initial investment back at the maturity date. If you do not have capital to invest directly into the government bonds, I suggest you invest in an exchange traded fund whose goal is investment in government bonds. An exchange traded fund (ETF) is a fund that is similar to a mutual fund BUT is traded on the stock market like a stock. Invest in these securities quarterly and watch your wealth grow.

For those of you who do not have a brokerage account feel free to navigate to the chapter on setting up a brokerage account. Once finish return here and follow these guidelines to build your government bond portfolio.

25%	iShares 1-3 Year Treasury Bond ETF
25%	iShares 3-7 Year Treasury Bond ETF
25%	iShares 7-10 Year Treasury Bond ETF
25%	iShares 20+ Year Treasury Bond ETF
	Mayberry Financial Basic Gov. Bond Portfolio 2018

Rebalance of the portfolio would need to be done at least annually. The percentage represents the cash value of the bond not the quantity of the bonds. At the end of the year you may have to buy and sell particular bonds to maintain balance. I suggest the quarterly investment interval to help keep your trading costs down. As you can probably now see there is no limit to the type of portfolio you can construct, for that reason I will not bore you with various portfolio allocations, instead if you have any questions about constructing a portfolio that meet your needs, use the contact information provided at the end of the book.

11 OPENING YOUR BROKERAGE ACCOUNT

Before you open your account you must know your investing goals. Without a goal it will be difficult to track your progress. You must determine <u>exactly</u> what you want to achieve by investing in the stock market. Is it for retirement? College fund? Income? Down payment for a house? It is <u>extremely</u> vital that you are clear on your goals before you begin your investment journey.

Opening your new investing account will be the next step. There are several to choose from, all with different fees, required deposits etc. What you need to focus on at this stage is what type of investing you will be doing. Features to consider would be things like will be the frequency of your investments and the monetary amount. You will find a broker that fits your needs after answering these types of questions. For example: If you are going to be making frequent trades, you may want to consider a brokerage firm that offer low to zero transaction commission costs. Online capability is a must. See below for some examples of brokerage firms.

- Charles Schwab
- Fidelity
- Merrill Edge
- E-Trade
- TD Ameritrade

I will now walk you through setting up your first brokerage account. I choose Fidelity to use as an example as it is user friendly and requires minimal time to setup. Before you begin be sure to have your bank account and routing number as you will need it initial fund your brokerage account and to use for future withdrawals and or automated funding features.

First visit their website and click "open

account"

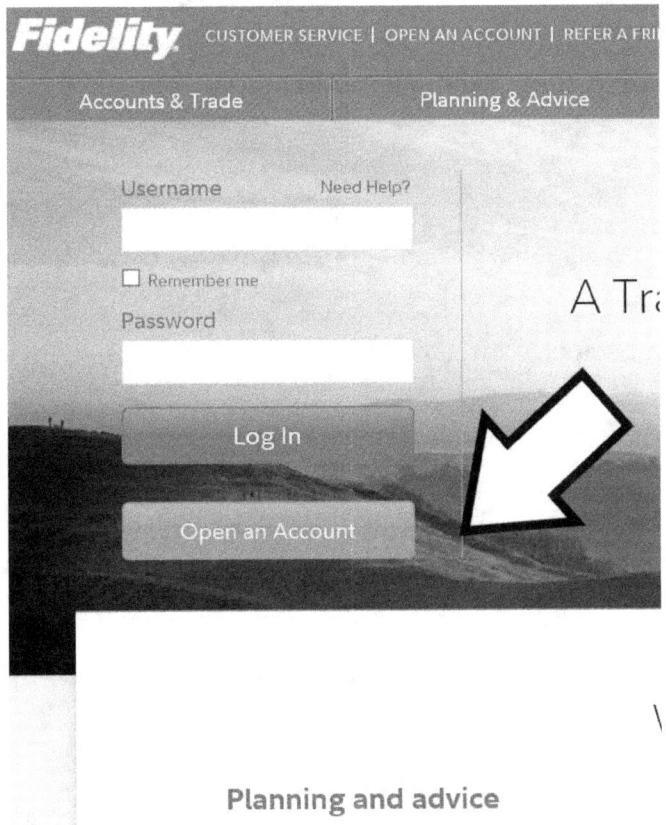

Planning and advice

On the next screen under brokerage and savings select "Open Now" underneath brokerage account.

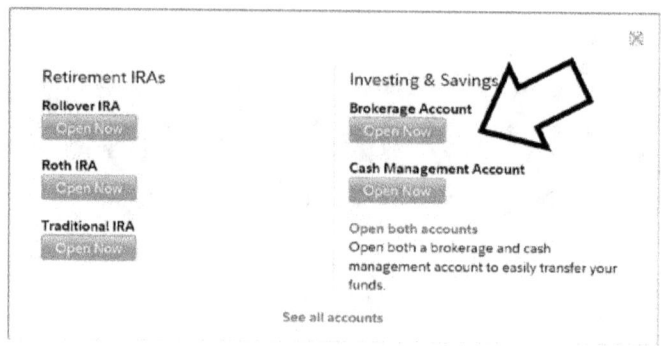

Next select your account type.

Now fill out the requested field boxes and press next.

Personal Information

In accordance with federal law, Fidelity Investments must obtain certain information to use in verifying your identity prior to opening your account.

All fields required unless otherwise noted.

Personal Information

	First	Middle (optional)	Last
Your Name	princeton		mayberry
Social Security Number			
Date of Birth	Month ▼		Month/dd/yyyy
Are you a U.S. Citizen?	Yes	No	
Phone			
Email			

Continue through the remaining pages to complete the account setup. You will be prompted if you would like to fund your account at this time. Enter the bank account routing and account number, select amount you would like to deposit and you're ready to start investing.

You also may want to setup your automatic investing and depositing features as well. I have found the most efficient way to have funds deposited into your brokerage account is to link it with your automatic deposit feature with your employer. To do this log into your account with your employer or you may have to speak with human resources if your company currently does not allow employees to edit their automatic deposit settings. While in the setting you will see and option to adjust the amount of money that is deposited into your checking account. Typically it will be 100%. Click edit and add in your new brokerage account. Depending on your company you may be able to send a set dollar amount to your brokerage account prior to your check going directly into your checking account. If not you can set the percentage to send to your brokerage account and have the reminder deposited into your checking account. Be sure to save the settings, your changes will take effect the following pay period.

Now your brokerage account will be automatically funded each pay period. The next step will be to setup automatic purchase setting of your selected mutual fund. If you are investing in stocks you will have to log into your account to process the investments. For those of you that prefer a completely hands off investment experience do the following to setup automatic investing into your chosen mutual fund.

Navigate to account settings and select account features.

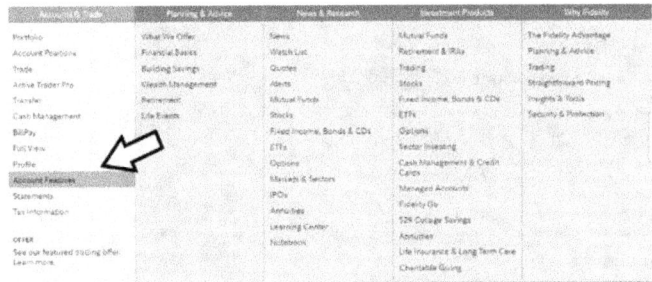

On the next screen under payments and transfers select automatic investments.

On the screen that follows you need to enter the name of the mutual fund and the dollar amount you would like to invest each period.

Set Up Automatic Investments

For Family Investments ▬▬▬▬▬▬▬▬

Transfer From
Your Brokerage Core Account

Transfer To

Mutual funds you own*	Amount
Choose a Fund ▾	$
	Total $ 0.00

* Funds with front end sales charges are ineligible.

Next you will need to setup the scheduling of your investments. If you are starting off with little investment capital I suggest a monthly investment schedule. For those of you with more capital I suggest a quarterly investment schedule.

Investment Schedule

Please allow at least two business days before your first automatic investment.

Day of month: 27 ▾

Frequency:

- ● Monthly
- ○ Quarterly - 1st month (Jan, Apr, Jul, Oct)
- ○ Quarterly - 2nd month (Feb, May, Aug, Nov)
- ○ Quarterly - 3rd month (Mar, Jun, Sep, Dec)
- ○ Create a custom schedule

Stop date:

- ● No stop date. (Automatic investments will be made on an ongoing basis unless you cancel schedule.)
- ○ Stop automatic investments after: [　　] / [　] / [　　] (mm/dd/yyyy)

The last feature I want you to setup is the automatic investment of dividend payments. Depending on your investments, you may receive a dividend payment from the companies you hold. Instead of having these payments sitting idle in your account, I would like them to be invested as well earning you more money and building your financial position and wealth in the process.

Navigate to account feature section.

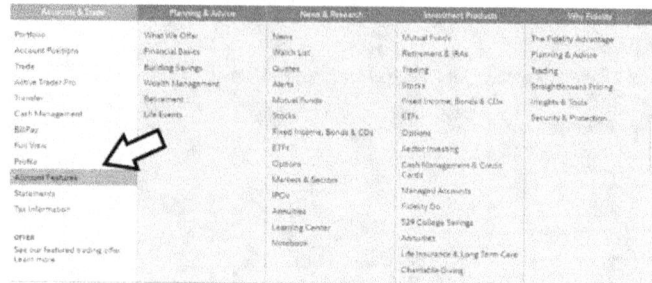

Underneath the brokerage and trading column, select dividends and capital gains.

On the next screen select update next to the investment you wish to update.

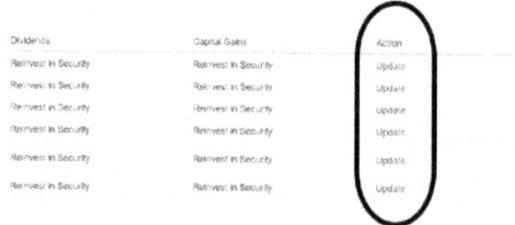

On the final screen click the bubble in the

middle that states reinvest in security. Be sure to check the two boxes below that this new setting will be applied to all your current positions in the investment and also any future positions you may take.

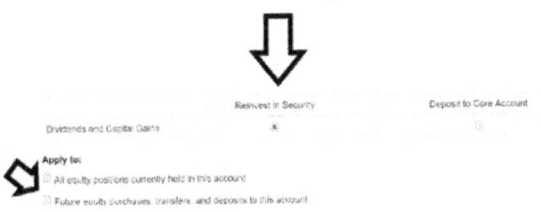

Now you are all set. You have taken a huge step in increasing your financial wealth and independence. I do recommend reviewing your account at least quarterly to see how you have increased your wealth. Again this automatic investment setup is ideal for those who desire a hands off approach to investing.

In your free time feel free to spend some time on your brokerage account exploring features and settings that it offers. While I used Fidelity in my example, these options will be available across all full services brokerage accounts, if not you may want to reconsider the firm.

For those of you that will be more involved in your investments, the brokerage firms typically provide investing new, graphs, tools and other information to assist you.

12 PROCESSING YOUR FIRST INVESTMENT

You know have an understanding of the stock market and how you can utilize it to meet your investment goals. We discussed a few strategies that will assist you in meeting these investment goals. Now it is time to process your first trade! I will walk your through processing your first trade using *Fidelity Investments*. Please be advised that while I am using Fidelity Investments for my example, other brokerage accounts may look different but the process is relatively the same. Also in no way am I endorsing Fidelity Investments.

Step 1: Select trade from your drop down menu

Princeton Mayberry

Accounts & Trade	Planning & Advice	News & Research
Portfolio	What We Offer	News
Account Positions	Financial Basics	Watch List
Trade	Building Savings	Quotes
Active Trader Pro	Wealth Management	Alerts
Transfer	Retirement	Mutual Funds
Cash Management	Life Events	Stocks
BillPay		Fixed Income, Bonds & CDs
Full View		ETFs
Profile		Options
Account Features		Markets & Sectors
Statements		IPOs
Tax Information		Annuities
		Learning Center
OFFER		Notebook
See our featured trading offer. Learn more		

Next your trade ticket below will appear

Help Me Trade ✕

Select an Account ▼

Transaction Type

Stocks/ETFs ▼

Symbol

Action

Select ▼

Quantity

＋ － Calculate
× ＝ Quantity

Order Type ⑦

Select ▼

Time in Force ⑦

Day ▼

Cancel **Preview Order**

- Learn more about Extended Hours Trading ⬈
- Important Disclosure Information ⬈
- Ask the Virtual Assistant your Trading questions ⬈

The ticket displays important information

related to completing your trade action. First select which account that will be processing the trade. Next you will need to choose the transaction type, that is what type of trade will you be processing (stocks, bonds, mutual fund etc.). Now select the quantity of the trade. In the action box you will choose trade. Take note of the other options available as in the future you may be utilizing them to complete trades. Now you will select your order type, the basic two types are:

Market Order – A buy or sell order to be executed immediately at the current market prices.

Limit Order – An order to buy or sell a stock at a specific price or better. A buy limit order can only be executed at the limit price or lower. A sell limit order can only be executed at the limit price or higher.

If the price is not of concern a simple market order will suffice, otherwise execute a limit order. The last option you need to select for your order is the time. The basic time frames would be a day order, which is only good for that day or a good til cancelled order, which will remain open until executed or cancelled by you. The last step involves you previewing the order to make sure all information is correct.

AT&T (T)

$30.52

Bid	$0.00
Ask	$0.00

AS OF 11/02/2018 5:00 PM ET

This order is to Buy 1 Share of T with a Limit Order (Day) at $30.51. This order will expire at 4:00 PM ET.

Estimated Order Value ████

Estimated Commission ████

Estimated Total Value ████

Please review order details. This order will not be placed until you select "Place Order".

Edit Order   **Place Order**

Important Disclosure Information ⬏

Take note of the estimated commission the brokerage may charge that will add to the total price of your order. If everything is correct, select the place order option and you have just completed your first trade. CONGRATULATIONS!

Princeton Mayberry

13 Employer Sponsored Retirement Accounts

The most popular form of investing by the working class in America would be through their employer sponsored retirement account, with the most popular being a 401k account. I always recommend to my clients to take advantage of this plan, which if used correctly can pay dividends in the future.

While I won't go into major detail about the 401k, I will discuss what I believe is the most important information regarding this type of account. First you will want to figure out if your employer matches your contributions to the fund. If they do, max it out up to that level. Since the money is deposited into the account before tax, it will help lower the taxes you pay. However the caveat is that when you withdrawal money in the future you will be taxed at the current tax rate. This is one of the reason why I do not recommend sending all you're saving or investment dollars into this account. I would like to also point out that the 401k is nothing more than a savings account. What happens when you spend all your money in your savings account? If all you had setup for your retirement was your 401k, you will be coming out of retirement sooner than later.

Now what is a 401k exactly? It is a mutual fund, defined by *Investopedia* as *"an investment vehicle made up of a pool of money collected from many investors for the purpose of investing in securities such as stocks, bonds, money market instruments and other assets"*. So in essence your money is pooled together with other investor's money and invested in the stock market. The fund is managed by a professional portfolio manager. You and the other investors in the fund pay this manager fees for their services. Similar to paying your financial advisor or broker for managing your portfolio. While this is not the optimal way to invest, I highly suggest that new investors start their investment careers with mutual funds.

Within these funds are several allocations of stocks and bonds and you choose where to invest? The types of bonds vary and if you do not select exactly what you want your money to be invested in, by default your money will be invested in a balanced portfolio option. Again when starting out this may be ok, however as your knowledge of the market increases you may need to adjust your holdings to reflect the current market status. You surely do not want to be heavily invested in stocks while the market is going into or currently in a bear market.

When you receive your quarterly statements *review the information.* You can see exactly how your current portfolio allocation performed and if you need to make changes. One of the positives of mutual funds is that you are not charged for making adjustments to your portfolio and you can make changes anytime. I urge you not to sit idle and not monitor or understand where and how your money is invested within your 401k or any other employer sponsored retirement account. Be active, be curious, and become wealthy.

If your company has chosen a reputable mutual fund company to host your 401k, you should have various free services available to you online. Setup up your online account access with the company. From there you have full access to your account. You can monitor and view your current balance, current allocation, current losses and gains. Let's take a look at a screenshot of 401k retirement account allocation.

Investment Allocations by Asset Class	Balance	% of Balance
● Short-Term Fixed Income	$0.00	
● Fixed Income	$339.28	
● Balanced/Asset Allocation	$7,063.03	
● Large U.S. Equity	$981.90	
● Small/Mid U.S. Equity	$1,204.20	
● International Equity	$94.90	
Total	$9,683.31	

If we do some simply math, this account is currently 73% invested in a balanced allocation account. However they are currently 0% invested in short term fixed income and 3.5% invested in fixed income. While I am not aware of what this individual's investment goal, a simple review of these figures tells me that readjustment is in order. For starters, within the balanced allocation you have all the classes included. So if they wanted a balanced approach they could simply invest 100% of their investment in that allocation and be done. It is this type of vital information that if the owner of this account was aware of, probably would have made a better decision about their allocation. I am positive the return on this allocation can be better than its current return.

However employees are not educated on monitoring their accounts. They are not informed on what a good return is or what to even expect out of an employer sponsored retirement account. I do not want you to be a part of this group of employees. Empower yourself and take control of your finances which includes your retirement account. If you have no desire what so ever to manage or be informed about your account invest 100% of you money into government bonds and forget about the account until retirement.

Princeton Mayberry

14 BRING IT ALL TOGETHER & EXTRAS

We have covered all the fundamental components of investing in the stock market. There are various financial vehicles that can be used to meet your investment goal. The purpose of this book is to expose you to the fundamentals of the stock market and how to use income generation strategies in the stock market. What I am out to cause with this book is to inform the working class of this great opportunity. The market does not care who you are, where you are from, nor how much you have. We all have a chance to receive the same rewards, and it does not require any formal education.

Remember the steps of getting started in the market. First be sure you are ready to invest. Perhaps a budget or personal finance overhaul is in order to organize yourself financially. I wrote a blog post about personal finance on my blog, seek it out for basic information and guidance on how to learn to manage your finances. Then determine your goal and what strategy will help you reach that goal.

At the end of this book I provide a few investment projects you can practice with your kids. I believe it is instrumental that the youth receive some form of financial education as it is not taught in public schools. Exposing them at an early age will teach them a lifetime skill of surviving in our capitalist country.

Be sure to take the portfolio allocation quiz as the first 100 readers will receive a free portfolio allocation.

Mayberry Financial is a finance advising firm that specialize in personal finance, wealth management and other related services. Checkout the website for more details.

Projects

Graph Assignment

Start off by talking to you your child and discovering the things they like or are interested in. Using that information pick the stock of the publically list company. Every weekend log onto the internet and pull up the graph of the selected company and do the following;

- Have you child draw the graph
- Have they explain what is happening on the graph
- Ask them, based on what they see would they like to save their money with the company

The purpose of this activity is to get your child familiar with reading and comprehending the basics of graphs and what they represent. As they mature and get older you can expose them to more advance exercises using the same graphs.

Savings Assignment

Begin by providing your child with a "see through" container that they can save their money in. I prefer "see through" because your child will be able to see their money visually anytime they want too, not to mention inspire them to save more as they notice it growing in size. Next you will need to purchase a basic notebook & pencil. To get started instruct your child to write their first & last name on the notebook. Also have them write "Deposit Book". Next let them decorate the notebook as they see fit. Now if they have stickers, let them also decorate the container as well.

Our goal with this assignment will be to teach your child the importance of saving and earning interest. The next step for you is to determine the allowance you want to pay your child for completing their chores. Don't worry it doesn't have to be substantial, it can be as simple as a dollar a week, you decide. Next you need to determine the amount of *interest* you want to pay to your child for saving their money instead of spending it. I recommend using 10% as it is easy to calculate, then do the following;

- Have you child open the notebook to

the first blank page

- Instruct them to write todays date
- Now you determine if they have completed their chores for the week to earn their allowance, if so you have them write that amount
- Next you explain to them that they earned interest (extra money) for saving their money. Instruct them to write the word interest and next to it the amount they earned
- Now have them count out the money, either by amount of coins or the actual dollar amount (depending on how advance your child is) and have them deposit the money in their container

EXTRA: If your child is at the stage where they can do addition, as they write additional pages have them add the amount each time, that way they will know exactly how much they have in their savings. If you child is not able to add yet do not worry, at the end of the saving period you take the deposit book and add up the pages. Then you add the money and see if they match.

Typing Assignment

The purpose of this assignment will be to get your child to work on their typing skills while learning about some of America's largest companies. To begin discover what companies your child are interested in. Next perform a search on a finance website (Yahoo Finance) to find the company profile. Copy and paste the profile into your word processor on your computer and then do the following;

- Instruct your child to type out the entire profile for the company. Feel free to break it up into chunks so it is easier for them to see and type
- Once done read through the passage your child has typed, advising of any mistakes made along the way
- Repeat with another company

Not only will your child work on their typing skills, hand and eye coordination but also learn about the companies that are industry leaders in our economy. The earlier they are exposed the better equipped they will be later on in life.

Portfolio Allocation Questionnaire

Answer the questions below and email answers to princetonmayberryfinancial@gmail.com to receive your personalized portfolio allocation.

On a scale of 1-10 what is your risk level? 10 being high level, 1 being low level

What is the goal of your portfolio?

Do you have a time limit for your portfolio? If so how long?

How much money each month will you be allocating to your investment account?

Do you have a personal interest in any industries?

Do you have any limitations on the types of securities you will use to achieve your goals?

Are you interested in leverage?

Will you be actively involved in your investment account or will you take the passive approach?

Do you have any additional information you would like to provide that would assist in creating your personalized portfolio?

Princeton Mayberry

ABOUT THE AUTHOR

Princeton Mayberry was born in Fresno CA.
He graduated from Fresno City College with
an Associate's Degree in Liberal Studies. He
began his financial education shortly
afterwards. He has been instrumental in the
starting of various small businesses and
provided financial consultation throughout
California. Princeton also has a background in
real estate investing.